Dedicated to my two boys, Jasper and Julian, whose bottoms I've wiped... I look forward to them doing that for me in about ten years or so.

I would also like to thank my Round Table, Patreon and Kickstarter supporters... especially:

Laura Gregg	John Reiger	Jennifer Pesek
Cindy Deichman	Lucia Port	Shawn
Katherine Freeman	Jack Valancy	Patricia Henry
Richard Padzerka	Matty Schwarzman	Ken Bachtold
Robert Gidley	Melissa A R Krause	Lucy Clark
Diane Simpson	Christine Galand	John Galleger
Terri Booth	C E Lawson	Robert Stiefel
Carol Fern Culhane	Barbara Diorio Fisher	Auntie Hallie
Andrew Green	Elizabeth A Gilliland	A T Green
Ann Wagner	David Emlen	Karen Davis
Alexandra Dorival	Kelly Gotschalk	Peter Mitchell
Maggie Frankel	Doug Seeley	Heather Daas
Fred Koch	Alex Haake	Andrea Denninger
My evil twin sister	Kathe Sandstrom	Lawrence Lane
Daniel Gilchrist	Tara Gallagher	Susan Vaillant
Oliver Tim Hirsig	James Hanley	Amy O'Malley
David Gustavson	Candace Koogler	Antje Boetus
John Holland	Judy Viertel	Summerlea
Johanna Trahan	Brek Renzelman	Terena Eisner
Jane Manning	Mary Zeugner	Steven L. Johnson
Becky White	Brian Harvey	Kenny Leung
Kenneth Gladden	Deborah Fowler	Sue Trowbridge
Joan Eisenstodt	Ralph Banks	Janece Moment
Timothy K.	Stephen Peters	Ben Mitchell
Fred Wright	David Gustavson	Jose Garibaldi
Rachel Rutledge	Dax Strife	A. M. Noble
Leslie Segelke	Wendy Hoffman	Esther Breslau
Richard Wells	John Louie	Rebecca Damsen
Sean Milroy	Eugene	Lori Llanillo
Gordon Lamb	Adam Beacham	Dawn Rutherford
Rand Bellavia	Anne McCarten-Gibbs	Sean Kinlin
Mick Shea	Tom O'Neill	Meg Winters
Allison Sharplin	Big Apple Mary	Win Bent
Ken Krepley	Peter Rubin	Genevieve C.
Sara Murray	Anna Wigtil	Cynthia Adkins
Ian Hagemann	Mick Shea	Melissa, Alex and Rafael
Manuel Burgos	Joe Roberts	John Beatty
Kellie Merrill	Marvin Hampton	Ernest Ondrias
Dawn McDonald	Minzoku Bokumetsu	David Patterson
Ricky Mendini	Eugene	J. Vincent

Peace, love, and lobstah rolls! ~KK

THE ETERNAL SUNSHINE OF THE SPOTLESS BEHIND

A **KNIGHT LIFE** COLLECTION

The Knight Life is distributed by Andrews McMeels for UFS
The Knight Life can be viewed at gocomics.com
Keef's other cartoons can be viewed at kchronicles.com
Subscribe and support Keef's work at www.patreon.com/keefknight

This book was designed by Jason Chandler.

Copyright © 2017 by Keith Knight

All rights reserved, except as pernitted under the U.S. Copyright Act of 1976, no part of this publication can be reproduced, distributed, or transmitted in any form or by any means, or stored in a database or retrieval system, without the prior written permission of Keith Knight. So there.

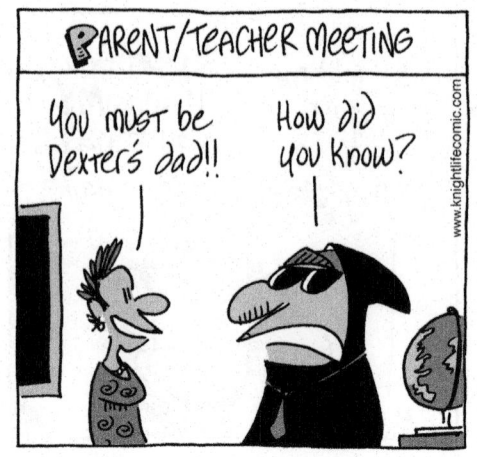

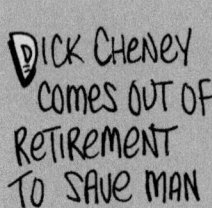
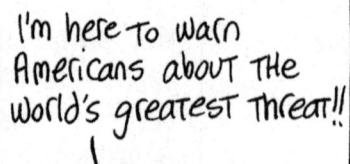

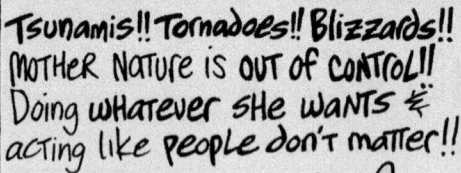
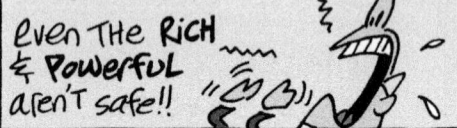

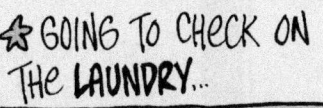

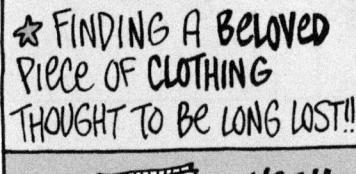

37

The U.S. postal service has raised its postage rates again!
IT'S AN OUTRAGE!!
I beg to differ!!
Whatchu talkin' bout Willis?
Name a better deal than the cost of a first class stamp!!
KEEF
For less than 50¢, you can send a letter door-to-door from the islands of Hawaii to the coast of Maine!!
Pacific ocean
5112 miles
Atlantic ocean
Your daily cup of coffee cost 4 times that much!!
So stop yer whining!!
Who paid you off?
Nobody!! I'm just a passionate advocate for mail enhancement!!
©2011 K. Knight/Dist. by UFS, Inc.
4/24
www.comics.com

Strip 1 (4/25):
- "The battle over Medicare cuts rages on!!"
- "How so?"
- "Activists face stiff opposition to the removal of Viagra from the list of covered prescriptions!!"
- "Of course they are!!"

Strip 2 (4/26):
- "Okay everyone!! We've got to figure out the best way of getting our 'Creativity Over Consumption' campaign off the ground!!"
- "Can we eat lunch first!!?"

Strip 3 (4/27):
- "Jimny Crickets!! There's a cop behind me flashing his lights!!"
- "OH NO!! He's pulling me over!!"
- "Relax, Kerstin.. There's a reasonable explanation why this is happening!! Remain calm.. say nothing stupid!!"
- "You're probably wondering why I pulled you ov--"
- "THE BODY IN THE TRUNK ISN'T MINE!!"

I can't believe I got stopped by the cops!!
Lookit all these people looking at me like I'm some sort of criminal!!
QUIT STARING OR I'LL GNAW YOUR EYELIDS OFF!!
Innocence & a heart of gold can be a burden!!
KEEF
www.comics.com
4/28
©2011 K. Knight/Dist. by UFS, Inc.

GET YOUR DAILY EXERCISE!!
RECENT RAIN? HEAD OUTSIDE & DO THE PUDDLE DODGE!!
ALL-W3T
WORKS LEGS
CALORIES BURNED: 420
CALORIES SOAKED: 1028
KEEF
©2011 K. Knight/Dist. by UFS, Inc.
www.comics.com
4/29

GET YOUR DAILY EXERCISE!!
KEEP THAT INEXPLICABLY DIFFICULT SHOPPING CART & WORK THOSE ARMS!!
Navels $3.-
SHAPES THIGHS, CALVES
WORKS ARMS, SHOULDERS
CALORIES BURNED: 720
MONEY BURNED: $75.00
KEEF
©2011 K. Knight/Dist. by UFS, Inc.
www.comics.com
4/30

One day at ye olde comic book convention
KEITH KNIGHT!! CHECK OUT MY COMIC!!
Sorry, man.. Gotta get back to my booth!!
OH SURE!! MR. BIG TIME CAN'T BE SEEN TALKIN' TO US LIL' FOLK!!
5/1
Allright... Let's see what you've got!!
Right on, bra!! You may not be as funny as you used to be, but I still respect your opinion!!
KEEF
This is pure bunk. A dung beetle wouldn't make a house out of this. My eyes burn at the illustrated atrocity I have just witnessed!!
www.knightlifecomic.com
PLOP
©2011 K. Knight/Dist. by UFS, Inc.
DID I MENTION YOU'RE MY BIGGEST INFLUENCE?!!
www.comics.com

42

Coupons You Can Use

"Extra Mix-In"
* Bearer entitled to one extra mix-in per treat
* Valid at any ice cream or frozen yogurt shop... (also: bars, pubs & saloons!!)

Value = priceless

"Shut Yer !@✻# Trap!!"
* Dear Sir/Madam... I understand this sporting event means LIFE or DEATH to you... ...but would it KILL YOU to refrain from the excessive use of PROFANITY in front of my five-year-old?

Value = priceless

"Bacteria-Free Flush"
How to use: Place cut coupon between hand & public toilet handle... push down.

* Entitles bearer to one bacteria-free flush (maybe)

Value: priceless

www.comics.com
We're home!!
©2011 K. Knight/Dist. by UFS, Inc.
?
SNIFF
5/9
www.knightlifecomic.com
Sniff
Are you reading Tragic mommy blogs again?
Maybe!!
KEEF

You got pulled over by THE Cops?
Yes!! IT was Terrible!!
www.comics.com
He asked me for my license and registration... wrote me a Ticket & sent me on my way!!
©2011 K. Knight/Dist. by UFS, Inc.
www.knightlifecomic.com
5/10
Is There anything more to THis story?
I KNEW YOU WOULDN'T UNDERSTAND!!
KEEF

So you got a traffic ticket-- Big deal!!
But I'm German!! I always follow THE rules!!
www.comics.com
5/11
Yet I made an illegal U-Turn! My moral compass has shifted!!
We all make mistakes!! No one got hurt!!
©2011 K. Knight/Dist. by UFS, Inc.
I reek of criminality!!
THAT'S Hippie deodorant from WHOLE FOODS!!
KEEF

This is Keith Knight!!
THE Keith Knight? Class of 1990?
Yup!!
This is your alma mater calling!! We're hoping we can count on you for a **generous donation** to the alumni association!!
Remember: The Alumni Association is here to serve **YOU!!**
Can you pay off my student loan?
KEEF
www.knightlifecomic.com
5/12
©2011 K. Knight/Dist. by UFS, Inc.
www.comics.com

It's almost noon!! Why didn't you wake me?
I've never seen you so deeply immersed in blissful slumber!!
I dreamt I was an air traffic controller!!
KEEF
www.comics.com
©2011 K. Knight/Dist. by UFS, Inc.
5/13
www.knightlifecomic.com

What happened to the breastmilk I had in the freezer?
That was breastmilk?
COMIX
Oh no-- What have you done?
I think we just invented the "Mom-sicle"!!
KEEF
©2011 K. Knight/Dist. by UFS, Inc.

"afternoon nap" by Kerstin
Now I lay me down to sleep...
I pray my kid won't make a peep...
But if he does before I wake..
My husband's life will be at stake!!
Guide to a Happy Baby
KEEF
5/15
©2011 K. Knight/Dist. by UFS, Inc.
www.comics.com

Special of the day?
Yup.. How much?
Free!!
Whaddaya mean, "free"?
Free!! Nada!! Zilch!! Zip!! You can donate whatever you can or walk away!!
?!?
PLOOF
Watch it, man!! I'm vegan!
www.comics.com
©2011 K. Knight/Dist. by UFS, Inc.
5/16

Dude!! I didn't get charged for my meal!!
That's the deal here, Gunther!!
No one is turned away for lack of funds!!
Man.. I hope none of my friends see me eating in a place like this!!
What? A vegan restaurant?
Nope!! A socialist restaurant!!
KEEF
www.comics.com
©2011 K. Knight/Dist. by UFS, Inc.
5/17

The food is great, huh?
Great, if it wasn't "pay what you can"!!
What's wrong with paying what you can afford?
IT'S UNAMERICAN!!
Perfect!! Your favorite food is Mexican, anyway!!
Dude, if I wanted free food, I'd be at my Mom's!!
KEEF
5/18

PAY WHAT YOU WANT CAFE
What are you doing?
There must be something wrong with this meal if I didn't have to pay for it!!
Donate ten bucks if it'll make you feel better!!
I'm gonna donate TWENTY!!
I'd rather complain about paying too much than worry about paying too little!!
KEEF
5/19
©2011 K. Knight/Dist. by UFS, Inc.
www.comics.com

I know you're just doing your "job."
Serving & protecting the innocent people of this neighborhood.
But could you follow me on Twitter, instead?
5/21
©2011 K. Knight/Dist. by UFS, Inc.
www.comics.com

Life's Little Victories
©2011 K. Knight/Dist. by UFS, Inc.
www.comics.com
FINDING ENOUGH QUARTERS TO DO THE LAUNDRY...
YES!!
..UNDER THE SEAT CUSHIONS OF YER COUCH!!
5/22
WAITING A DAY TO PURCHASE AN AIRLINE FLIGHT...
KEEF
Yes!!
Sale!! 189.00 RT
AND THE PRICE DROPS BY HALF!!
THE SKY-SCRAPER ELEVATOR YER RIDIN' IN...
YES!!
GOES FROM TOP TO BOTTOM, WITH NO STOPS!!
BRINGING THE WRONG INGREDIENT HOME FOR A RECIPE...
SCHLLURP!!
!!!
..& IT MAKES THE DISH EVEN BETTER!!
FLICKING ON AN NHL PLAYOFF GAME IN OVERTIME..
GOAL!!
..JUST BEFORE YER TEAM SCORES THE GAME-WINNER!!

What are you giggling for?
I just hooked you up!!
I photoshopped your new book into this Bin Laden death photo so it looks like it was the last thing he was reading!!
When you pick your jaw off the floor...
!?!!
A "Thank you" would be nice!!
KEEF
5/23
www.comics.com
©2011 K. Knight/Dist. by UFS, Inc.

WHY DID YOU PHOTOSHOP MY BOOK WITH BIN LADEN?!
It's great publicity, bra!!
Do you realize how many **eyes** are viewing that photo at this very moment?
Yes!! The C.I.A., Al Qaeda, T.S.A, The Taliban & my **MOTHER**!!
See? You can't **pay** for that sort of coverage!!
KEEF
5/24
www.comics.com
©2011 K. Knight/Dist. by UFS, Inc.

Is there a problem, officer?
Yes, cartoon man!! There is!!
I saw your latest book in that Bin Laden death photo on the internet!!
You got it all wrong!! It was photoshopped in there!!
I don't care where he bought it-- **YOU'RE GOING TO GUANTANAMO!!**
5/25
www.comics.com
©2011 K. Knight/Dist. by UFS, Inc.

Something just brushed against my leg!!
That's the internet troll I hired to clear my name on the web!!
©2011 K. Knight/Dist. by UFS, Inc.
5/26
Ever since Gunther photoshopped my book into that Bin Laden photo, my honor's been **besmirched** all over the blogosphere!!
www.knightlifecomic.com
www.comics.com
So you hired a troll to work under the table?
SHHH!! He thinks it's a bridge!!
KEEF

Dude!! You hired an internet troll?!!
Darn right I did!!
www.comics.com
©2011 K. Knight/Dist. by UFS, Inc.
5/27
I've been getting **slammed** ever since you photoshopped my book into that Bin Laden death photo!!
I get it!! But why waste money when you can troll for yourself!!
Oh no... I would **never** stoop so low!!
KEEF
www.knightlifecomic.com

©2011 K. Knight
What happened to the troll you hired to defend your honor online?
Tap
Tap
Tap
www.comics.com
©2011 K. Knight/Dist. by UFS, Inc.
Gunther taught me how to be my own internet troll, so I gave him the ax!!
That explains the blood stains on the carpet!!
KEEF
5/28
www.knightlifecomic.com

OHMIGOSH!! LOOKIT THE POOR LITTLE BIRDIE!!

STATE OF THE UNION
It's no surprise we're in such dire straits financially!!
A third of our population doesn't work, can't speak the language, is dysfunctionally illiterate, & livin' off the dole!!
A third of our population is only 4 months old!! And so what if he likes bananas!!
www.comics.com
5/30
©2011 K. Knight/Dist. by UFS, Inc.
KEEF

Wow!!
What?
©2011 K. Knight/Dist. by UFS, Inc.
5/31
According to the New York Times, human hair has become the item to steal for thieves across America!!
Really?
www.comics.com
I'd like to report a robbery!!
KEEF

More mail for you!!
©2011 K. Knight
You've been getting an awful lotta packages lately!!
6/1
You're not planning an escape, are you?
KEEF
www.comics.com

54

Deadlines.. Radiation... Bills.. The economy.. Health insurance.. Tornadoes.. Tsunamis..
The death of print.. Death of parents... Dwindling savings... Suicide... Indifference.. Oil spills..
War... Murder ...e-coli... Birthers.. Gas prices... Red Sox/Yankees.. Wall St. bonuses.. Corporate welfare..
Cancer.. Autism.. Dirty water.. Innocent death row prisoners... Racism.. Sexism.. Domestic abuse.. Old age.. Lost hair... Broken dreams..
P.T.S.D... Guns.. Texting while driving.. Lying politicians.. Little yappy dogs.. Another Trans-former mov--
CHOMP
AUGH!!
ga!!
www.comics.com
©2011 K. Knight/Dist. by UFS, Inc.
www.knightlifecomic.com
KEEF
6/5

WHAT are you WATCHING?
THE SyFy CHANNEL!!
www.knightlifecomic.com
ANOTHER one of THOSE "DINOCROC VS. MONSTERGATOR" MOVIES?
BETTER THAN THAT!!
©2011 K. Knight/Distributed by Universal Uclick for UFS
6/6
Tiger MOTHER VS. OCTO-MOM!!
KEEF

The SyFy CHANNEL PRESENTS: Tiger MOTHER VS. OCTO-MOM!!
I don't believe IT!!
www.knightlifecomic.com
What began as a simple playdate...
..ended in mayhem!!
©2011 K. Knight/Distributed by Universal Uclick for UFS
6/7
Words are exchanged... Parenting skills questioned..
Can someone read my brain cells their last rites?
KEEF

"Tiger MOTHER VS. OCTO-MOM" was excellent!!
©2011 K. Knight/
6/8
My favorite part was when Tiger MOTHER CHEWED off one of OCTO-MOM'S arms & made her kid play VIOLIN WITH IT!!
Distributed by Universal Uclick for UFS
My favorite part was when Gerard BUTLER walked in WITHOUT a SHIRT on & asked for a massage!!
www.knightlifecomic.com
That wasn't in THE movie!!
Really? I must've dozed off!!
KEEF

You watched "Tiger Mother vs. Octo-Mom" last night? Which version? They made two!!
www.knightlifecomic.com
One to appease Western audiences, where the Octo-Mom wins...
6/9
Distributed by Universal Uclick for UFS
And an Eastern version rarely seen here, where the Tiger Mother wins!!
Honestly, I think we all lost!!
KEEF
©2011 K. Knight/

I was driving down the wrong side of the road?
Yes ma'am!!
www.knightlifecomic.com
My S.d.9 navigational system told me to go this way!!
Your what?
6/10
©2011 K. Knight/
My S.d.9 navigational system!!
I think it's installed upside-down, ma'am.
KEEF
Distributed by Universal Uclick for UFS

The Wifey Picks a Movie
Rent -a- Movie
How about this one?
Are you nuts?!
Tornado Terror!!
www.knightlifecomic.com
What's wrong with it?
I thought you didn't like scary movies!!
©2011 K. Knight/
6/11
Funny.. I don't remember "Twister" being that scary!!
It is now!!
Rent -a- ovie
Tornado Terror
KEEF
Distributed by Universal Uclick for UFS

BUTCHERED AMERICAN SAYINGS BY MY GERMAN WIFE
Don't count your chitterlings until they're hatched!!
I'm NOT ready to throw up the towel!!
We're killing TWO rats with one stick!!
KEEF
SIR-- DON'T THROW STONED IN GLASS HOUSES!!
6/12
If the glove don't fit, you must quit wearing it!!
?
©2011 K. Knight/Dist. by UFS, Inc.
IT AIN'T OVER TIL THE CAT LADY SINGS!!
They're so cute, I'll never tell!!
www.comics.com

Who dat?
It's Keith's bud!! I'm here for poker night!!
The "man" shut down my online poker site, so I'm making the transition to real-life poker!!
You might wanna wear more than a thong!!
Really? It's what I'm used to wearing when I play!!
KEEF
www.knightlifecomic.com
©2011 K. Knight
Distributed by Universal Uclick for UFS
6/13

Gentlemen!! I wanna thank you for letting me join your poker night!!
You'll no doubt find us online poker nuts not much different than your average poker-mon!!
QUACK
Though I do have a tendency for flatulence whenever I get a good hand!!
KEEF
©2011 K. Knight
Distributed by Universal Uclick for UFS
www.knightlifecomic.com
6/14

Hey!! I wanna talk to you about that guy you sent to my poker night!!
UH OH!!
He showed up **nude**, cut the cards with a **meat cleaver**, & consulted a **psychic** to make bets!!
Sorry!!
Au contraire!! Got any more rubes to send my way?
$ $ $
KEEF
www.knightlifecomic.com
Distributed by Universal Uclick for UFS
©2011 K. Knight
6/15

COP VS. FIREMAN!!

You pole dancers are outta luck this upcoming golf tourney!!

I'll have you know our team has been practicing for this event all year!!

We'll be shootin' birdies & eagles all day long!!

I'll alert PETA to stage a protest!!

COP VS. FIREMAN!!

A bookie I arrested sez the police are favored 4 to 1 in this year's golf tourney!!

How can that be?

We've won every year except 2006!!

That was the year I shot a hole-in-one!!

Pumping a slug into a golf cart doesn't count!!

COP VS. FIREMAN!!

I'd wish you good luck, but it wouldn't be sincere!!

Don't feel bad when we crush you on the golf course.. you'll always have your dalmation!!

I'll see you at the 19th hole!!

Wait!! The first bogey's on me!!

©2011 K. Knight
Distributed by Universal Uclick for UFS
SON!! I BROUGHT SOME-THING HOME FOR YOU!!
Whoa!! LookiT all Those vinyL records!!
COST me Ten bucks!!
OOH!! ETTa James!! Cole Porter!! Miles Davis!! TiTo Puente!!
Are They good?
KEEF
Uh oH.
WhaT?
These are all unplayable!! Look aT all THE ScraTcHes!!
6/19
ScraTcHes? Aw, man...
Never buy vinyL from a fLea markeT!!

Hello?
Hi!! This is your lucky day!!
Distributed by Universal Uclick for UFS
Our records show that your passive income status & unique demographics qualify you for a program that could pay up to $30,000!!
6/20
www.knightlifecomic.com
That's the nicest way I've ever heard someone say "You're broke, desperate & willing to do anything for money!!"
Thanks!!
KEEF
©2011 K. Knight

Clovis... You ever hear about the "Adopt-a-Prisoner" program?
Sure!!
It was implemented after the Supreme Court ordered the state to purge 30,000 low-risk prisoners from the state pen!!
©2011 K. Knight
6/21
The state is paying families $30,000 to house a felon for a year--a fraction of what it costs the state to imprison them annually!!
!!!
www.knightlifecomic.com
How "low-risk"?
No worse than Gunther!!
Oh dear!!
KEEF
Distributed by Universal Uclick for UFS

Adopt-a-Prisoner!!
This is where you'll be sleeping!!
Distributed by Universal Uclick for UFS
In a closet?
I know it's a bit cramped...
But it's all we've got!!
6/22
©2011 K. Knight
When are the other three showing up?
How overcrowded was that prison they had you in?
KEEF
www.knightlifecomic.com

ADOPT-A-PRISONER!!

UH OH.. Here comes a fellow felon!!

Should I be worried about you two breaking out in fisticuffs over something meaningless like gang affiliation?

≥Gasp≤ It's Yankee fan!!

Red Sox fan!! I thought I smelled sumthin'!!!

Should I be worried about YOU?

GRRRRRR...

6/23

Oh my goodness!! What happened?!!

Your husband ran into a Yankee fan!!

Is he all right?

Better shape than the Yankee fan!!

GLggL BLXfft SCHLife

What did he say?

He said he broke out his two heavy hitters: "Big Papi" & "Carlton Fist!!"

YESH!!

6/24

Hello?

Hello!! This is your unlucky day!!

Our records show you got into a fight in the company of your adopted prisoner, which disqualifies you from the program!!

You owe us $30,000!!

Whoa!! College flashback!!

6/25

63

Distributed by Universal Uclick for UFS
In preparation for the final Harry Potter film, I am consuming each previous installment through the miracle of 3-D!!
But the previous films weren't in 3D!!
Yours truly has invented a 3-D format far superior to the conventional 3-D used in today's films!!
KEEF
6/26
I watch each film on my laptop while simultaneously listening to the audiobooks & reading the novels!!
The multi-format input provides a true 3-D experience!!
Yeah, demented, deranged & delusional!!
©2011 K. Knight

65

MUNCH MUNCH
How'd you sleep?
Terrible!! Spiders were biting me all night long!!
On my arms!! On my legs!! Even on my-
That was me!!
KEEF
©2011 K. Knight
Distributed by Universal Uclick for UFS
www.knightlifecomic.com
6/30

Where should I put you while I vacuum the floor?
WHIRRRRRRR
KEEF
www.knightlifecomic.com
©2011 K. Knight
Distributed by Universal Uclick for UFS
7/1

Hippie!!
Geek!!
Sellouts!!
©2011 K. Knight/ Distributed by Universal Uclick for UFS
7/3
Hoodlum!!
Thug!!
Communists!!
KEEF
Simpleton!!
Elitist!!
Vegetarians!!
GANG MEMBERS!!

www.knightlifecomic.com
Distributed by Universal Uclick for UFS
POP
7/4
HAPPY INDEPENDENCE DAY!!
(Bee) Careful!!
KEEF
©2011 K. Knight

Arrr!! Welcome to Pirate Supper Theater!! I be Stink-beard, your waiter for the evening!!
www.knightlifecomic.com
Tonite's specials include the final Harry Potter film, the upcoming Mission Impossible Movie & the latest Lady Gaga CD!!
©2011 K. Knight
Distributed by Universal Uclick for UFS
I think they've gone overboard with the piracy theme!!
KEEF
7/5

PIRATE-THEMED RESTAURANT
Excuse me, Mr. Stink-beard?
ARRR!!
www.knightlifecomic.com
7/6
My husband went to the restroom 30 minutes ago & never returned... Could you check on him?
Aye, matey!!
©2011 K. Knight
Distributed by Universal Uclick for UFS
He's been taken hostage by Somalis.. Here are the demands if you want him back!!
KEEF

69

There are more of us than there are of you, a sea of devotion in red, white & blue...
We're lovable losers, despair at our core til the Yankees collapsed in 2004...
We stay til the end, even during a rout, If it wasn't for us you'd never sell out
Make one trip to Fenway, & you'll understand, the resolute resilience of a true Red Sox fan!!
www.knightlifecomic.com
©2011 K. Knight
KEEF
Distributed by Universal Uclick for UFS
7/10

You're THE guy WHO never cleans up after His dog!!
Whoops..I don't have a bag!!
Here!! I don't ever wanna see THE sidewalk in front of my apartment littered WITH dog waste again!!
okay!!
7/11
©2011 K. Knight
Distributed by Universal Uclick for UFS
KEEF

PICK UP AFTER YOUR DOG!!
What's **next?** Will my Doberman have to wear a **doggie diaper?**
©2011 K. Knight
Then **what?** Will I have to teach him how to use a **TOILET?!!**
7/12
It's a slippery slope, I tell ya!!
Yes!! It **is** slippery... **SO CLEAN IT UP!!**
Distributed by Universal Uclick for UFS
KEEF

PICK UP AFTER YOUR DOG!!
Why? I never had to do it when I wuz a kid!!
©2011 K. Knight
Back in THE day, **rampant canine scat** was **revered** in literary circles..only **recently** being **vilified** by today's liberal media!!
PICK UP AFTER YOUR DOG!!
Winnie THE Pooh wasn't always a bear, you know!!
Distributed by Universal Uclick for UFS
7/13

PICK UP AFTER YOUR DOG!!
Do you know what you SHOULD be doing instead of bugging me?
Distributed by Universal Uclick for UFS
7/14
You SHOULD be holed up in your apartment inventing a machine that'll convert all this dog waste into bio-degradable fuel!!
Do you realize how much dough you'd make?
PICK UP AFTER YOUR DOG!!
BROWN IS THE NEW GREEN!!
KEEF
©2011 K. Knight

An independent study found Zimbabwe's voter rolls contain 2.5 million names of dead or fictional voters!!
Distributed by Universal Uclick for UFS
The voter register includes tens of thousands of citizens supposedly over 100 years old...
... in a country where the average life expectancy is 49!!
Never under-estimate the Zombie vote!!
KEEF
7/15

ZIMBABWEAN ZOMBIE VOTER
©2011 K. Knight
Name?
Unngh
VOTER CHECK-IN
Wow!! That's the thousandth "UNNGH" to check in today!! You come from a large family!!
grunt
7/16
Distributed by Universal Uclick for UFS
WANT... B-B-BRAINS!!
"Brains"? Don't think we have any brains on the ballot!!
Mugabe
Mugabe
M. Ugabe
KEEF

Life's LITTLE Victories
FINDING $5 PARKING TWO BLOCKS PAST THE $20 LOT!!
Yes!!
$5
7/17
Distributed by Universal Uclick for UFS
THE CONCERT TICKETS YOU WERE GIVEN TURN OUT TO BE TOP CHOICE SEATS!!
KEEF
Down THis way!!
yesss...
THE OPENING BAND, WHOM YOU'VE NEVER HEARD BEFORE, KICKS MAJOR BOTTOM!!
I got more RHymes THAN THE Bay's got Hippies!!
©2011 K. Knight
THE HEADLINER PLAYS EVERYTHING YOU WANT TO HEAR, EVEN THE OBSCURE!!
Anybody wanna hear "PARTY UP"?
YES!!
YOU GET LUCKY IN THE PARKING LOT AFTER THE SHOW!!
OoH look!! A five dollar bill!!
www.knightlifecomic.com

How's THE world's 2nd greatest air guitarist doing?
My manager sent me my upcoming tour SCHEDULE!!
Distributed by Universal Uclick for UFS
2 nights in Afghanistan.. 3 shows in Yemen.. 2 in Syria.. 3 in Somalia.. 2 in NORTH Korea...
©2011 K. Knight
7/18
...and a 21 night stint in Folsom State prison!!
I'm beginning TO THink he doesn't have my best interests in mind!!
KEEF

7/19
©2011 K. Knight
GUNTHER...
GUNTHER...
GUNTHER
Sez here too much coffee can cause some drinkers to hallucinate!!
Ya Think?
KEEF
Distributed by Universal Uclick for UFS

All THE advice I hear regarding THE economy is TO **downsize** your workforce!!
©2011 K. Knight
But what happens if you're a self-employed freelancer? How do you downsize when you're the sole employee?
7/20
Distributed by Universal Uclick for UFS
Have you considered amputation?
KEEF

Distributed by Universal Uclick for UFS
ONE DAY AT COMIC-CON
YOU!!
WHY WON'T YOU TELL US YOUR BABY'S NAME?!!
IT'S DRIVING ME CRAZY!!
©2011 K. Knight
WHAT ARE YOU AFRAID OF?!!
KEEF
KEITH KNIGHT
7/21

What's that guy doing?
He's holding his breath until I tell him our son's name!!
©2011 K. Knight
KEITH KNIGHT
7/22
How long has he been doing it?
17 minutes by my watch!!
Should we call a medic?
Why? Are you sick?
KEEF
Distributed by Universal Uclick for UFS
KEITH KNIGHT

COMIC CON!!
What happened?
You were holding your breath & passed out!!
A young woman dressed as "slave Leia" came by & gave you MOUTH-TO-MOUTH!!
7/23
Ohmigosh!! And it never would've happened had you told me your son's name!!
Thank you, Keith Knight!! Thank you!!
Distributed by Universal Uclick for UFS
Why did you lie to him like that?
Comic-Con is where fantasies come true!!
KEEF
©2011 K. Knight

I'm at Comic-Con in San Diego right now!!
Distributed by Universal Uclick for UFS
Are you Keith Knight?
Yup!!
Sigh
What's wrong?
©2011 K. Knight
Have you ever been super-excited to meet somebody & totally disappointed when it finally happened?
Once!!
Keef
It was a reader... Burdened with over expectation!!
By Keith Knight
The Knight Life
Is your wife or Gunther around?
My wife is.
Can you tell her she has my sympathy?
She'd rather have your credit card-- Buy my book!!
7/24
That went better than most!!

I remember THE first Time I changed our baby's diaper!!
I was shocked to see how much He resembled a plucked, uncooked chicken!!
ORGANIC CHICKEN
Did IT make you WANT To quit eating poultry?
IT made me WANT TO eat THE baby!!
7/25
©2011 K. Knight
Distributed by Universal Uclick for UFS
KEEF

Are you giving me a TICKET in a supermarket parking lot?!!
You're car is in TWO SPOTS!!
SECURITY
There was an S.U.V. in a compact space THAT forced me To park THAT way!!
Relax!! This Ticket is only a warning!!
They're no longer content in Their fake cars & uniforms.. Now they're giving out fake Tickets!!
7/26
©2011 K. Knight
Distributed by Universal Uclick for UFS
KEEF

How is THAT new Therapist of yours?
I've never had anyone probe so deep into my past before!!
She had me write down my medical History... Then SHe asked about my family history...
Then SHe Took my laptop & searched my browser history!!
7/27
©2011 K. Knight
Distributed by Universal Uclick for UFS
KEEF

OoF!! What's THAT smell?!!...
That's my new odorant!!
©2011 K. Knight
Don't you mean DE-odorant?
Oh no!! Deodorants are passé!!
STENCH FOR MEN Back Kitchen
7/28
StenchTM for Men comes in a variety of odors!!
STENCH FOR MEN ZOO
STENCH FOR MEN FISHING BOAT
STENCH FOR MEN SLAUGHTER HOUSE
Distributed by Universal Uclick for UFS
Well, IT STinks!!
To you, IT STinks.. To women, I smell employed!!
KEEF

©2011 K. Knight
7/29
TWEET
BLACK SHOOTS TWO!!
Distributed by Universal Uclick for UFS
What'd I get called for?
Fragrant Foul!!
KEEF

WHAT THEY SAY VS. WHAT THEY MEAN
Distributed by Universal Uclick for UFS ©2011 K. Knight
SNIFF Looks like somebody pooped again!!
"If you think I'm changing another diaper today..."
I got IT!!
7/30
If you happen to see any chocolate while you're out...
"Two bars, 72% dark, with nuts & raisins.. or don't come home at all!!"
KEEF

Heal The Bay released their annual beach report cards!!
www.knightlifecomic.com
Our two favorite spots received "F" grades!!
Distributed by Universal Uclick for UFS
How can people say they love the beach, yet treat it so poorly?
KEEF
On top of the list for garbage found on coastlines: CIGARETTE BUTTS!!
7/31
Do smokers think cigarette butts are so small that they're not really litter?
FLICK!
©2011 K. Knight
THE ONLY BUTT I WANNA SEE ON THE BEACH SHOULD BE IN A BATHING SUIT!!
OR NOT!!
WWW.HEALTHEBAY.ORG

80

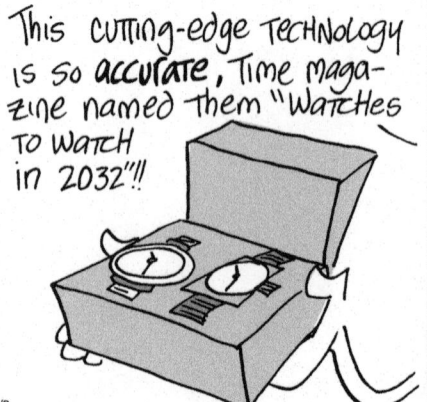

HIPSTER ICE CREAM SHOP

What's the wildest thing you've got?

"Sundae brunch"!

Buttermilk ice cream in a waffle cone, covered in maple syrup, topped with a fried egg, a stick of butter, & two pieces of bacon!!

You expect people to eat that?

We suggest slathering it directly onto your bottom!!

Breast milk ice cream? I'll try some!!

Cup or cone?

Is that a trick question?

The ice cream shop is now selling breast milk ice cream!!

I wasn't sure you'd like it so I bought you a cup!!

I see you got the Double D's!!

In their own commemorative plastic jugs!!

©2011 K. Knight
My!! What a beautiful child you have!!
Thanks!! You Too!!
How old is your son?
WHoa--Wait!! Did I mention anything about gender?
Distributed by Universal Uclick for UFS
I'm raising "Bowl" to be non gender-specific!!
KEEF
NOBODY knows the sex of my child!! That way they can wear pink or blue & won't be Teased!!
8/7
Won't they be Teased for wearing a bird's nest on their head?
Another awkward moment at the playground?
My client refuses to talk to the media!!

83

84

I forgot my keys & Kerstin's out with the boy!!
Do you have a credit card?
www.knightlifecomic.com
Distributed by Universal Uclick for UFS
Yup!!
How 'bout American Express?
©2011 K. Knight
Since 1988!!
Thanks!!
KEEF
But you'll never get in!! It's double bol--
POP
B-But... HOW?
Membership has its privileges!!
8/14

www.knightlifecomic.com
Dexter!! Can you help me with this new cell phone?
Sure!!
8/15
Distributed by Universal Uclick for UFS
I finally broke down & got one after they removed the last payphone in the neighbor-hood!!
Trouble is... I'm all thumbs when it comes to this new-fangled technology!!
That's actually a **GOOD** thing!!
KEEF
©2011 K. Knight

I appreciate you setting up my new cell phone for me, Dexter!!
No prob!!
©2011 K. Knight
Distributed by Universal Uclick for UFS
Who knows how much I woulda spent hiring "Nerd Herd" or "Geek Squad" to help me out!!
Okay!! You're all set!!
8/16
www.knightlifecomic.com
What's with the chicken satay & the slider?
I down-loaded some free apps for you!!
KEEF

Who were you talking to?
The cartoonist.. He needed help with his cell phone!!
©2011 K. Knight
Hmmm.. That's the 3rd person who's asked you this week...
UH OH.
Distributed by Universal Uclick for UFS
12 watt
www.knightlifecomic.com
TECHNOLOGICAL HELP $50
THE 6 YEAR OLD IS IN
KEEF
8/17

www.knightlifecomic.com
TECHNOLOGICAL HELP $50
THE 6 YEAR OLD IS IN
My kids bought me this cell phone with web access!!
8/18
My wife & I can't read the text on this little screen!! What are we to do?!!
Distributed by Universal Uclick for UFS
©2011 K. Knight
TECHNOLOGICAL HELP $50
THE 6 YEAR OLD IS IN
Take two tablets & call me in the morning!!
KEEF

TECHNOLOGICAL HELP $50
Next!!
THE 6 YEAR OLD
Upon retirement, the military gave me a mini super-computer!!
©2011 K. Knight
8/19
The SuperHawk 3000TM has a HUGE herd of RAM, 1000 milliliters of TORQUE & a 1700 ELEPHANT MEMORY!!
Distributed by Universal Uclick for UFS
ECHNOLOGICAL ELP $50
So what's your problem?
E 6 YEAR OLD
How do I put those little smiley faces on the end of my emails?
KEEF

TECHNOLOGICAL HELP $50
THE 6 YEAR OLD IS IN
I'd like to leave my cards at your booth!!
8/20
NOLOGICAL ELP $50
"Eve's Apple". What kind of business is it?
6 YEAR
Discreet services for the Un-P.C. professional!!
Distributed by Universal Uclick for UFS
NOLOGICAL HELP $50
I'll run this by my Dad & see what he thinks!!
6 YEAR IS IN
Please do!! And tell him he gets a 25% discount!!
KEEF
©2011 K. Knight

DROOK
©2011 K. Knight
8/21
KEEF
There it is!! A block away!!
DROOK
Two for THE featured exhibit!!
18 dollars!!
Distributed by Universal Uclick for UFS
DROOK
WOW!! COOL!!
NO PHOTOS

89

20 minutes straight!!
WAAAHHHH
©2011 K. Knight/Distributed by Universal Uclick for UFS
35 minutes straight!!
WAAAHHH
WEEHOO WEEHOO WE
!!!
8/25
The Fire Department saved us again, today!!
KEEF

Every time I put him on my shoulders, he gums the top of my head, trying to taste my brains!!
MUNCH MUNCH
©2011 K. Knight
Makes me think he's got a little of zombie in his genes!!
GNAW GNAW
8/26
Is there something regarding your family that you haven't told me about?
Gum Gum
Distributed by Universal Uclick for UFS

What color is it?
Green & stinky!!
©2011 K. Knight
8/27
That explains his cranky mood!!
It sure does!!
FLIP
PLOP
Distributed by Universal Uclick for UFS
Baby poop is the original mood ring!!
KEEF

Strip 1 (8/29):
- "I mean, seriously!! Why would the News Corp. phone-hacking scandal be limited to just the U.K.?"
- "News Corp. owns media all over the world!! Surely they share ideas, resources, logistics & business techniques!!"
- "Sounds like paranoid gibberish to me!!"
- "Really? This coming from 'conspiracy guy'?"
- "Even conspiracy guy knows crazy when he hears it!!"

Strip 2 (8/30): RETURN OF CONSPIRACY GUY!!
- "I'm APPALLED that you would suggest that the News Corp. phone-hacking scandal could possibly be larger than it is!!"
- "Why would News Corp. jeopardize its otherwise STELLAR reputation by hacking beyond the tens of thousands of cell phones it's already hacked within British borders?"
- "To be fair & balanced to their U.K. victims?"
- "The owners of Fox News want none of that!!"

Strip 3 (8/31):
- "If people have nothing to hide, they needn't worry about their cell phone being hacked!!"
- "There are so many more important stories than the News Corp. scandal... like starving babies in Africa!!"
- "Have you ever seen the configuration of a British cell phone? They're practically begging to be hacked!!"
- "Are you reading talking points off of your smartphone?"
- "It's a new app from News Corp.!!"

Why are **YOU** so paranoid about the phone-Hacking scandal?
What are **YOU** Trying to Hide?
Distributed by Universal Uclick for UFS
9/1
Do you have some kind of dirty **TWEET** floatin' around, cartoon man?
©2011 K. Knight
I'm startin' to think you're on the News Corp. payroll!!
Someone had to class up the joint, post-Glenn Beck!!
KEEF

Okay, so whadda we gotta get?
3 PENS PENCILS MARKERS
According to this email: Pens, note-book, a backpack...
©2011 K. Knight
Pencil sharpener, desk, office chair...
Distributed by Universal Uclick for UFS
Copy machine, wall clock, P.A. system, school bus...
Wait a sec... **Who** are we buying these school sup-plies for?
9/2
KEEF

Geez Louise!! I don't remember "back-to-school" shopping being this **HARSH!!**
FICE COPIER
STUDENT DESK
PENS
©2011 K. Knight
Gone are the days of one pen, one pencil & a Mead Trapper Keeper!!
Distributed by Universal Uclick for UFS
Excuse me... Spare chalk? Spare CH--
I'm **broke**, man!!
OFFICE COPIER
STUDENT DESK
Wait-- Was that guy asking for chalk?
That's my 2nd grade teacher!!
9/3
KEEF

93

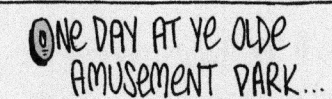

BACK TO SCHOOL!!
My name is Mrs. McKittrick & I am your new Home Economics Teacher!!
Gone are the days of **sewing** & baking **cookies!!** This new Home Economics class will reflect Today's modern household!!
We'll be focusing on food stamps, foreclosures, unemployment, & how to avoid calls from collection agencies!!
KEEF
©2011 K. Knight
Distributed by Universal Uclick for UFS
9/5

Dex!! How's the new school year treating you?
My Home Economics class is a Trip!!
All we do is talk about Home Loan defaults & unemployed adult children returning to live in their parent's home!!
Wow!! Home Eck sounds really depressing!!
It's no longer "Home Ec." It's just "Heck"!!
KEEF
©2011 K. Knight
Distributed by Universal Uclick for UFS
www.knightlifecomic.com
9/6

Don't forget the parent/teacher meeting at school today!!
Aw, man!! Do I hafta go?
Yes you do!! Don't you want to take part in your child's education?
Last time I went, I was bullied by a fellow parent!!
You're gonna need a better excuse than that!!
How 'bout I haven't been vaccinated?
KEEF
www.knightlifecomic.com
Distributed by Universal Uclick for UFS
9/7

Dexter!! What are **YOU** doing at the Farmers Market?
Ditching a Parent/Teacher meeting at my kid's school!!
www.knightlifecomic.com
I dropped outta that school 30 years ago!! What if they're trying to get me back in to finish?
Distributed by Universal Uclick for UFS
©2011 K. Knight
9/8
You think this meeting is some sort of drop-out sting operation?!!
The school mascot is a yellow jacket!!
KEEF

Distributed by Universal Uclick for UFS
You're probably wondering why I stopped you!!
©2011 K. Knight
9/9
I'm avoiding a parent/teacher meeting at my kid's school!!
Really? So am I!!
www.knightlifecomic.com
Butchie!! Dexter!! Why aren't you at school right now?
It's Mr. Williams, the truant officer!!
He's still **ALIVE?!!**
KEEF

RUDY RAY MOORE ELEMENTARY
Here we are!! Our old alma mater!!
PARENT/ TEACHER MEETINGS ALL DAY
©2011 K. Knight
Are you ready to step into the way-back machine?
www.knightlifecomic.com
9/10
Distributed by Universal Uclick for UFS
What do you miss more? Sloppy Joes or Tater Tots?
Wedgies!!
KEEF

Life Little Victories
Distributed by Universal Uclick for UFS
9/11
THUMBING A TEXT WITHOUT EVER HITTING THE WRONG KEY!!
YES!
*Never happens
WHEN SOFTWARE THAT'S SUPPOSED TO TAKE 2 HOURS TO DOWNLOAD...
KEEF
DING
YES!
.. ONLY TAKES FIVE MINUTES!!
©2011 K. Knight
AFTER WATCHING RERUNS OF AN OLD SHOW FOR DECADES..
Ginger?
Yes, Mary Ann?
Is the water warm?
..YOU COME ACROSS AN EPISODE YOU'VE NEVER SEEN BEFORE!!
DRINKING COFFEE WHILE DRIVING...
..JERKING TO A QUICK STOP...
ERRR
..AND THE SPILLAGE LANDS ON YOUR SEAT BELT, NOT ON YOUR CLEAN SHIRT!!
SO BUCKLE UP!!
YES!!

THAT TIME OF YEAR AGAIN
TUMBLE
PLUNK
©2011 K. Knight
STUMBLE
SPLAT
SLIP
Distributed by Universal Uclick for UFS
It must be fall!!
KEEF
9/12

What are you reading?
An in-depth article on Dolly Parton!!
PARADE
It's an up-close look at her two enormous talents!!
PARADE
DOLLY!
9/13
Distributed by Universal Uclick for UFS
©2011 K. Knight
PARADE
Singing & songwriting!!
KEEF
PARADE

Got him!!
Distributed by Universal Uclick for UFS
He's big!!
Thank you!! Been workin' out!!
9/14
©2011 K. Knight
That wasn't a compliment!!
KEEF

98

Distributed by Universal Uclick for UFS
WRITER'S BLOCK
DEAD-LINES
KNOCK KNOCK KNOCK
BATH TIME!!
©2011 K. Knight
KEEF
9/18
SMACK
Never hurts to kiss a little butt on the job every once in a while!!

Panel 1 (9/19):
- "Hey man!! The Wi-Fi signal in here is **weaker** than the Brazilian roast!!"
- "Both had better get stronger when we return or my colleagues & I might do something **drastic**!!"
- "Like write negative reviews on yelp!!"
- ≡Sigh≡ Gangs sure ain't what they used to be!!

Panel 2 (9/20):
- "Who are those dorky-looking dudes with the tablets & laptops?" "Gang members!!"
- "'N.W.A.' goes around shaking merchants & customers down for protection money against hackers & viruses!!"
- "N.W.A.?" "Nerds with Aptitude!!"

Panel 3 (9/21):
- "You're probably wondering why I pulled you over!!"
- "I have reason to believe your son may be involved in a local gang!!" *GASP*
- "Are you crying?" "Tears of joy!!"

You THink my son is a gang member?
The "Nerds with Aptitude" have been actively courting him for MONTHS!!
www.knightlifecomic.com
©2011 K. Knight
Those who refuse To join N.W.A. are The Targets of harrassment, abuse, even gunshots!!
9/22
Distributed by Universal Uclick for UFS
GUNSHOTS?!!
OH yeah!! They'll gang up on you in "Call of Duty"!!
KEEF

POINDEXTER JUNIOR!! YOU GET IN HERE RIGHT THIS MOMENT!!
9/23
A local peace officer has expressed concern THAT you might be involved with The Notorious local gang "Nerds with Aptitude"!! Is THIS True?
Distributed by Universal Uclick for UFS
Sorry To disappoint you...
AUGH!! I KNEW IT SOUNDED TOO GOOD TO BE TRUE!!
©2011 K. Knight
KEEF

Son!! You might want to reconsider joining THis gang!!
Gangs just aren't my THing!!
Distributed by Universal Uclick for UFS
The "Nerds with Aptitude" sounds SO MUCH like your THing, IT's absurd!!
I want To use my intelligence for good!!
©2011 K. Knight
9/24
Still can't get him To join The dark side?
I'm still Trying To figure out where I went right!!
KEEF

LET me SHOW you THIS ongoing experiment I've been doing!!
©2011 K. Knight
I purchased THIS fast-food hamburger on September 13TH, 1992!!
Wow!! Looks like you got it yesterday!!
KEEF
9/25
I had planned on incorporating THE results into a performance ART piece about CHemical preservatives in fast food...
Distributed by Universal Uclick for UFS
...but I THink I'm JUST gonna TOSS IT in a blender & use IT as an anti-aging cream!!

You leave for Brooklyn Tomorrow!! ..
What airline are you flying?
Derry-Air!!
©2011 K. Knight
DERRY-AIR!!
That's that Super-Hip European airline!!
What's so Hip about it?
Distributed by Universal Uclick for UFS
Purple strobe lights in the cabin!! Onboard Karaoke!! Clothing optional seating!! Free Vodka Gimlets!!
What about children?
9/26
Kids fly in the cargo Hold with the Pets!!
OOH!!
KEEF

©2011 K. Knight
Is this the check-in counter for Derry-Air?
Yep!!
9/27
Distributed by Universal Uclick for UFS
Are you gonna check me in?
When I'm done checking you out!!
KEEF

If you're flying Derry-Air, you have the option of by-passing regular security...
Distributed by Universal Uclick for UFS
9/28
..and submitting to an enhanced search involving Swedish & Asian massage (For a $75 fee)...
©2011 K. Knight
That explains how they can charge so little for the flight!!
KEEF

Did you ring THE attendant call button?
I have a question!!
Distributed by Universal Uclick for UFS
9/29
©2011 K. Knight
I really appreciate the in-flight Karaoke machines...
But am I the only one nervous about THE next 3 passengers doing songs by Buddy Holly, Lynyrd Skynyrd & Aaliyah?
KEEF

Sir!! We've landed at J.F.K... You can de-plane now!!
I AIN'T GOIN'!!
9/30
Derry-Air was SUCH a perfect airline experience, THE rest of my trip is guaranteed to be a letdown!!
Distributed by Universal Uclick for UFS
SO I AIN'T GOIN'!!
I THought we stopped serving nuts onboard years ago!!
KEEF
©2011 K. Knight

Your comic strip got replaced!!
Oh no!!
CALENDAR
©2011 K. Knight
AUGH!! THE "GOOD OL' DAYS"!!
WHAT'S THAT?
CALENDAR
The Good OL' Days is a 150-year-old comic strip widely regarded as THE zombie of newspaper cartoons!!
10/1
Distributed by Universal Uclick for UFS
The zombie of newspaper cartoons?
IT JUST WON'T DIE!!
KEEF
CALENDAR

Panel 1
"Did you find that site I wanted you to look for?"
"What site?"

Panel 2
"The site for that Time Travel Mart!!"
"OH!! I'm sorry!! I started searching my favorite craft site & totally lost track of what I was doing!!"

Panel 3
"There's a medical term for what ails people like you!!"
"What's that?"

Panel 4
"Forg-Etsy!!"
"Ooo!! Crotcheted egg-warmers!!"

Checking in!!
I.D. & credit card, please!!
10/3
Federal Law requires me to inform you that this hotel now charges for services that formerly came free with the room!!
©2011 K. Knight
Distributed by Universal Uclick for UFS
Are you gonna tell me what they are?
For a $3 service fee!!
KEEF

HOTEL HELL!!
Concierge!! What's taking the elevator so long?
You gotta put a credit card in the slot!!
10/4
I have to **pay** to use the elevator?!!
Part of our **new fee structure!!** You can always take the stairs!!
©2011 K. Knight
Distributed by Universal Uclick for UFS
My room is **7 floors up!!** You're **worse** than the airline companies!!
Name **one** airline that gives you **seven** flights for **5** dollars!!
KEEF

I can't believe all the new fees this hotel is charging!!
10/5
How can I enjoy myself if I'm constantly being **nickel & dimed?**
~~FREE~~ Coffee
©2011 K. Knight
BUSINESS SERVICES
Hmmm.. Not bad!!
You know it's ugly when the hotel's business service rates start looking like a bargain!!
KEEF
Distributed by Universal Uclick for UFS

There are no pillows on my bed!!
We have 'em down here behind the desk!!
©2011 K. Knight
All right-- What's it gonna cost me?
Nothing!! They're absolutely free!!
Distributed by Universal Uclick for UFS
10/6
Thanks!! What a pleasant surprise!!
It's the least we can do-- (considering all the bed bugs!!)
KEEF

A **curse** on these new fees hotels are pushing on their customers nowadays!!
Five bucks for use of the elevator? **Seven** for toilet paper? **Two dollars** per remote control click? **TWO MUCH!!**
10/7
T.V. OR NOT T.V.? THAT IS THE QUESTION!!
©2011 K. Knight
KEEF

Checking out!!
We hope you had a great stay here in Brooklyn!!
Just let me run your credit card for any service fees you may have accrued during your visit!!
©2011 K. Knight
10/8
Distributed by Universal Uclick for UFS
Wow!! You managed to avoid every annoying little fee we've implemented!! How did you do that?
I CRASHED ON A PAL'S COUCH IN QUEENS!!
KEEF

Psst!! Wanna see something neat?
Look what happens when I stuff gummy bears, honey & love into this grinder..
Distributed by Universal Uclick for UFS
Ohmigoodness!! A PUPPY!!
KEEF
crank crank
It's a puppymill!! Pretty neat, huh?
crank crank
That's not a puppy-mill!!
©2011 K. Knight
10/9
A puppy mill is a mass dog breeding facility that cares more about profits than puppies!! Most mills are overcrowded, filthy..with inadequate food, water & health care!!
How barbaric!! They treat those dogs like..like...HUMANS!!

COUPONS YOU CAN USE
©2011 K. Knight
Distributed by Universal Uclick for UFS
10/10
"ONE FREE TOLL"
✲ ENTITLES BEARER TO ONE FREE PASS THROUGH ANY TOLL BOOTH
$4 TOLL
CASH OR FAST TRAK
$4 TOLL
CASH OR FAST TRAK
cut here
*IF YOU DON'T DRIVE, ONE FREE TOLL-HOUSE COOKIE!!
COUPON
KEEF

COUPONS YOU CAN USE
©2011 K. Knight
Distributed by Universal Uclick for UFS
10/11
"DIBS ON LAST OUTLET"
✲ BEARER ENTITLED TO LAST REMAINING OUTLET IN CAFE, AIRPORT, OR OTHER PUBLIC SPACE.
COUPON
cash value = priceless
KEEF

COUPONS YOU CAN USE
©2011 K. Knight
Distributed by Universal Uclick for UFS
10/12
cut here
"PERSONAL FOUL"
coupon
✲ BEARER RESPECTFULLY ASKS THAT YOU TONE DOWN THE PERFUME D'ODOR...
SPRITZ SPRITZ
..BECAUSE ONLY ONE LETTER SEPARATES "SCENT" FROM "STENCH"
cash value = priceless
cut here
KEEF

Coupons You Can Use

"Please Don't Call On Me Today"
★ Despite circumstances well within their control, bearer asks that you **not** rely on them for **anything** remotely important.

Good for one 24-hour period

Valid in all class, conference & board rooms.

cash value = priceless

"Re-Butterfication"
★ Entitles bearer to a second hit of "butter"-flavored substitute....

...after half-way point is reached in popcorn tub.

cash value = priceless

"One Free Ice Cream"
★ Bearer will gladly pay you Tuesday for an ice cream today!!

Life's Little Victories!!
10/16
☆ Threading the needle..
Yes!!
On the very first try!!
☆ Getting back to your parked car..
Wait!! I'm here!!
Lucky!!
..Just before it gets a ticket!!
Distributed by Universal Uclick for UFS
☆ That beat-up lookin' C.D.
Frankie say "relax"
Keef
..Plays perfectly!!
☆ Picking up a tennis racket after a decade...
Yes!!
Two handed
..And hitting a perfect backhand!
©2011 K. Knight
☆ Pulling yer baby in a wagon to & from the store..
..& he never climbs/falls out!!
☆ Pickin' yer dad's football card by team mascot...
But... How?!!
Never under-estimate the Lions!!
..And winning 10 outta 10!!

112

OCCUPY MAIN STREET!!
WEALTH-CARE 4 $UM!
Why are you so concerned about the well-off?
Shouldn't we be asking the rich to pull themselves up by their own bootstraps?
What about all the people the rich hire to pull up their bootstraps for them?
WEALTH-CARE 4 $UM!
KEEF
Distributed by Universal Uclick for UFS
10/21
©2011 K. Knight

The rich have taken over Main Street!! Demanding Wealthcare for sum!!
And the police have shown up!!
Here comes a cop!! D'ya think he'll do anything?
Is that pepper-spray in his hand?!!
Fresh pepper for your caviar, sir?
Thank you, boy!!
KEEF
Distributed by Universal Uclick for UFS
10/21
©2011 K. Knight

I'm home!!
Did you hear about the billionaire protest downtown?
I was there 'til the cops showed up & started beating people!!
Really? I can't imagine the rich being brutalized!!
I didn't say they beat the protesters!!
KEEF
©2011 K. Knight
Distributed by Universal Uclick for UFS
10/22

©2011 K. Knight
IS THAT a dead bird?
10-4!!
LICE LINE DO NOT CROSS POLICE LINE DO
Who would commit SUCH a heinous act?
A feral cat!!
10/23
Distributed by Universal Uclick for UFS
A feral cat is a sort of untamed, wild version of THE domesticated housecat!!
KEEF
"They roam America's streets, parks & alleys, unchecked, killing millions of birds each year!!"
Nuggets
"THE feral cat population continues to benefit from a HIGHLY, SANITIZED portrayal of THE blood-THIRSTY beasts from THE 1960's!!"
You're blaming Hanna-Barbera?
We call 'em "Hanna Barbaric" down at THE station!
POLICE LINE DO NOT CROSS POLICE LINE DO

My bank is gouging me with fees!!
You should switch to mine!!
Distributed by Universal Uclick for UFS
It's a fee-free religious-themed bank that is gaining popularity across the country!!
Fee-free? How can that be?
10/24
©2011 K. Knight
Technically, they're considered tithes!!
JESUS Saves
BA
NO FEES!!
KEEF

Welcome to Jesus Saves!! The first religious-themed financial institution!!
Distributed by Universal Uclick for UFS
10/25
Do you serve all denominations?
Of course we do!!
©2011 K. Knight
Tens, Twenties, Fifties, & Hundreds!!
KEEF

Since we're still a church, "Jesus Saves" pays little to no taxes!!
It's the safest a financial institution could ever be!!
JESUS Saves
ANK
NO FEES!
©2011 K. Knight
Prayer while waiting in line is encouraged!! And you can confess your sins while making a deposit!!
10/26
Distributed by Universal Uclick for UFS
By making "Jesus Saves" your bank, money won't be the only thing that will be saved!!
KEEF

How is a religious-themed bank gonna help me save more money?
The higher your balance, the closer you are to Heaven!!
©2011 K. Knight
The lower it is, the closer you'll be to the-- ahem other place!!
10/27
Distributed by Universal Uclick for UFS
So you do it through fear & guilt!!
If it ain't broke, why fix it!!
KEEF

THE OTHER 1%
Distributed by Universal Uclick for UFS
The chief sent me to answer questions regarding your safety during Halloween Night!!
©2011 K. Knight
How can we stop Wall Street protesters from showing up with Trick-or-Treaters?!!
Stop whining about taxes & stop paying C.E.O.s 400 times the average worker!!
WHAT?!!
Just joking!! You can shoot 'em if you want!!
KEEF
10/28

THE LITMUS TEST
Sir... You've been on record saying your were against hand-outs...
Yes, ma'am!!
©2011 K. Knight
10/29
Distributed by Universal Uclick for UFS
So if elected president, is it safe to say you'd ban Trick-or-Treating on Halloween?
Can you remind me what the voting age is?
KEEF

ALTERNATIVES TO HALLOWEEN CANDY
by a new dad
10/30
©2011 K. Knight
Banana
BRIDES-MAIDS
D.V.D.
ICE TRAY
SHOT GLASS
Distributed by Universal Uclick for UFS
AVOCADO
KEEF
Hockey Tickets
FLASH DRIVE
Beef Jerky
BAND-AID
ADHESIVE BANDAGES
FLASK
THE KNIGHT LIFE
COMICS!!

TRICK OR TREAT!!
Where are your papers?
What?
No handouts til you can prove you're a citizen of these United States of America!!
??
You said there was a lot of candy in Alabama!!
I said there were a lot of NUTS!!
©2011 K. Knight
10/31
Distributed by Universal Uclick for UFS

Didja hear the news? The City Zoo got foreclosed on!!
Lions & Tigers & bears & moose & albatrosses are getting kicked to the curb!!
How 'bout bats?
Even bats!!
I thought they were leftover Halloween decorations!!
KEEF
Distributed by Universal Uclick for UFS
11/1
©2011 K. Knight

You're probably wondering why I stopped you!!
A bunch of wild zoo animals are loose on the streets!! A few of 'em attacked some PETA protesters a half block away!!
It got UGLY.
I think I wanna SEE that!!
Ten bucks gets you past the yellow tape!!
KEEF
Distributed by Universal Uclick for UFS
11/2
©2011 K. Knight

WALL STREET IS FULL OF BULL!!
OCCUPY OR DIE
11/3
THEY'RE LION TO ALL OF US!!
OCCUPY OR DIE
Distributed by Universal Uclick for UFS
HEY!! WHY IS EVERYBODY RUNNING? IS IT THE PIGS?!!
OCCUPY OR DIE
©2011 K. Knight
STAY & BEAR WITNESS TO WHAT THE MAN HAS COMING TO HIM!!
KEEF

AUTUMN!! What are you doing in a meat dress? There are LIONS about!!
Sacrificing myself!! But they ran right past me!!
Am I so unappealing that I can't even get eaten by LIONS while wearing a meat dress?!!
Here's your problem!!
11/04
©2011 K. Knight
Distributed by Universal Uclick for UFS
This dress is 100% Seitan!!
WHAT?! Damn lady sold me a KNOCK-OFF?!!
KEEF

WILD KINGDOM COME!!
IT'S Clovis on THE phone!! SomeTHing jumped on his back & tackled him in THE street!!
©2011 K. Knight
Distributed by Universal Uclick for UFS
He sez it's clawin' at his back & biting his ear!!
Is it a wombat?!!
Is it a dingo?!!
I Think it's a cougar!!
PURRRR
11/5
KEEF

had planned to draw an amazing strip, with 3-D, unicorns & sound.

Fueled with laughter pain, & regret, it was really quite profound.

Thanks a lot, lady!!

But as I left the Post Office I heard & felt a *SLAM*. Some lady let the front door close, on my drawing hand!!

A simple little "sorry" is all she *never* said. Now the only thing that I can draw is the back of her foolish head!!

Psst!! Kerstin!!
!!!
I'm sorry... Please take us back!!
Netflix guy, again?
Yup!!
I'll throw in 20,000 Qwikster T-shirts!!
11/7
www.knightlifecomic.com
Distributed by Universal Uclick for UFS
KEEF
©2011 K. Knight

Clovis!! I made a HUGE mistake!!
OMG!! Reed Hastings, CEO of Netflix!!
Splitting Netflix in two AND raising fees were terrible moves!!
Don't listen to him!! He'll do or SAY ANYTHING to get me back!!
"IN YOUR eyes..."
Whoa-- He's good!!
©2011 K. Knight
Distributed by Universal Uclick for UFS
11/8
KEEF
www.knightlifecomic.com

Reed Hastings of Netflix left a voicemail!!
Again?
He sez we shouldn't let his two bad decisions drive us away from the convenience Netflix provides when it comes to renting movies!!
He's offering free copies of Kevin Smith's "Cop Out" if we rejoin today!!
They say bad decisions come in threes!!
www.knightlifecomic.com
Distributed by Universal Uclick for UFS
©2011 K. Knight
11/9
KEEF

We have credible info THAT you've received a bomb in THE mail Today!!
!!!
www.knightlifecomic.com
11/10
©2011 K. Knight
Distributed by Universal Uclick for UFS
Think hard: Who hates you?
GOSH--Where do I begin? Mimes!! Canadians!! Hippies!!
A DVD of Kevin SMITH'S "Cop Out"!!
Our worst fears confirmed!!
OH--And Kevin SMITH fans!!

How's THE employment search going, AUTUMN?
I applied To a couple of places looking for holiday help!!
www.knightlifecomic.com
11/11
Distributed by Universal Uclick for UFS
©2011 K. Knight
excellent!! SOUNDS like THE economy is looking up!!
NOT really...IT was for a soup KITCHEN & a suicide hotline!!
KEEF

WHERE'S GUNTHER?
How's your air-guitar world Tour?
Terrible!!
©2011 K. Knight
11/12
every Time I Try To get paid for a gig, THE dictator who invited me gets overTHrown!!
I'm in line now To see if I can avoid getting ripped off by another deadbe--
!!!
Distributed by Universal Uclick for UFS
GunTHer's in Libya!!
KEEF
www.knightlifecomic.com

Mr. Knight.. Can you step out of the line, please?
UH OH!!
Distributed by Universal Uclick for UFS
I just wanted to tell you that it doesn't look good!!
©2011 K. Knight
I've seen this before & I'd say you've got 2 to 3 months tops!!
KEEF
11/13
I just wanted to prepare you for the worst...
I'm sorry.
THAT'S A LITTLE OVER-THE-TOP FOR A LOW-BALANCE CHECKING ACCOUNT, DON'TCHA THINK?!!

In anticipation of my imminent demise, I'm gonna order a personalized coffin from overseas!!
In Ghana, skilled artisans create coffins designed to look like planes, cars, beer bottles...whatever!!
Distributed by Universal Uclick for UFS
Weren't you just whining about not having enough to pay rent next month?
!!!
11/14
I DON'T CARE WHAT YOU SAY!! I'M GHANA DO IT!!
KEEF
©2011 K. Knight

Distributed by Universal Uclick for UFS
How do I look?
Like you're going to a funeral!!
I AM going to a funeral!!
Then you look perfect!! GO!! You're late!!
11/15
Don't smile!! People will misinterpret it!!
SHOVE
Have a miserable time!!
KEEF
©2011 K. Knight

C'mon people!! I wanna see a lot more emotion coming from you!!
We're talking DEATH here!!
©2011 K. Knight
I'd better hear wailing once the dog comes in, or I'm storming out of this CHURCH!!
Distributed by Universal Uclick for UFS
Wow!! I don't recall funeral directors like that back east!!
Welcome to Los Angeles!!
KEEF
11/16

Who lit this casket? It's horrendous!!
Are all funeral directors like that in L.A.?
Yup!!
©2011 K. Knight
Many use funeral directing as the first step towards becoming a film director in Hollywood!!
Seriously?
11/17
Distributed by Universal Uclick for UFS
Funerals have all the hall-marks of an Oscar-winning film: Death. Drama. Emotion...
...and an out-of-control budget!!
KEEF

This funeral is absolutely ATROCIOUS!!
©2011 K. Knight
The pacing is wrong!! The music is terrible!! The overall tone is soul-draining!!
11/18
Distributed by Universal Uclick for UFS
I should be directing this funeral!! I'd show these idiots how to lay someone to rest!!
I'd put the FUN back in funeral!!
I bet!!
KEEF

I've never heard about film directors getting their start directing funerals!!
Oh yeah!!
FUNERA PARK
11/19
In 1973, a bespectacled young filmmaker directed the funeral of a So-Cal surfer who was eaten by a shark!!
©2011 K. Knight
Two years later, Steven Spielberg made "Jaws"!!
AND the surfer's name was "Indiana Jones"!!
KEEF
Distributed by Universal Uclick for UFS

Does anyone know who THAT guy is in THE hot TUb?
I Thought YOU knew him!!
I Thought YOU did!!
Distributed by Universal Uclick for UFS
11/20
Well.. He's had THAT hot TUb all To himself THE whole Time!!
KEEF
Well.. I ain't gonna get in There with him... He's like, THE CREEPIEST guy in THE world!!
©2011 K. Knight
Stay creepy, my friends!!

I don't know, Doctor!! He's been like THis all day!!
11/27
Mouth agape!! Eyeballs popping out of His Head!!
www.knightlifecomic.com
..And staring into his hand!!
You want me To WHAT?
Look on THE floor around him?
©2011 K. Knight
Distributed by Universal Uclick for UFS
GASP You're right!!
It's THE first bill for his new cell phone!!
KEEF

COCKROACH!!
Distributed by Universal Uclick for UFS
There's a COCKROACH in THE KITCHEN!! DO SOMETHING!!
FUNNY TIMES
You're not Trying To catch it with a drinking glass, are you?
We gotta use THAT!!
KEEF
You're not gonna smash it, are you? You'll spread roach eggs all over!!
©2011 K. Knight
12/4
You're not gonna spray poison, are you? We can't have our baby breathing THAT STUFF!!
Now I understand why cockroaches have been around for so long!!

ANIMAL HUSBANDRY!!
ANIMAL HUSBANDRY!!
HIDE YOUR KIDS!! ANIMAL HUSBANDRY IS BEING PRACTICED RIGHT NOW!!
KEEF
I knew THis would happen once THey allowed same-sex marriages!!
©2011 K. Knight
12/11
"Animal Husbandry is THE agricultural practice of breeding & raising livestock!!"
Seriously? THAT'S IT?
≈SigH≈ Knowledge may be power, but ignorance is way more fun!!
Distributed by Universal Uclick for UFS

VISITING MY DAD
©2011 K. Knight
We've reached Vegas!!
How can you tell?
12/12
The foreclosure signs are all Neon!!
BANK OWNED
BANK OWNED
KEEF
Distributed by Universal Uclick for UFS

How's it goin', Pop?
Terrible!!
CASINO
Something's wrong with the plumbing, so my water is shut off for the next 24 hours.. AND, 3 of my neighbors just got foreclosed on!!
12/13
©2011 K. Knight
The whole neighborhood's underwater, yet I can't even take a shower!!
KEEF
Distributed by Universal Uclick for UFS

©2011 K. Knight
Wow!! This news story claims that it costs a quarter million dollars to raise a kid from birth til 18!!
I believe it!!
VEGAS NEWS
Distributed by Universal Uclick for UFS
Speaking of which- where's my grandson?
Don't you mean your "250 grand" son?
VEGAS NEWS
12/14
KEEF

Why don't you move your family to Las Vegas? You can buy the house next door for a song!!
BLLFFTT
Are you s-serious?!!
Vegas is a wonderful place to raise a kid!!
The only thing between here & the local casino is an adult bookstore!!
WHAT? You got a problem with literacy?!!
INO
Distributed by Universal Uclick for UFS
12/15
©2011 K. Knight
KEEF

VEGAS!!
Is that a new casino?
Yeah--A high-end D.C. themed joint!!
©2011 K. Knight
D.C.? As in District of Columbia?
Yep.. It's got replicas of the Bill of Rights, the Oval office, even the M.L.K. Memorial!!
12/16
Wow!! Can we get in & check out the lobby?
Only if you're a lobbyist!!
Distributed by Universal Uclick for UFS
KEEF

I thought you were boycotting the circus because of animal abuse!!
I was!!
Two tix!!
Distributed by Universal Uclick for UFS
12/19
Since being penalized for beating elephants, circus officials have come up with a **more entertaining** alternative!!
Which is..?
Republicans!!
KEEF

I gotta admit.. Substituting Republicans for elephants was a brilliant move by the circus!!
Ha!! Check it out!!
Everyone's attacking Romney!!
Why are all those clowns just standing around doing nothing?
They're Democrats!!
KEEF
©2011 K. Knight
12/20
Distributed by Universal Uclick for UFS

Wow!! The circus IS a lot more fun when they beat politicians instead of elephants!!
What was your favorite trick they were forced to do?
I loved how many feet Perry could put in his mouth!!
My favorite was Gingrich juggling all his ex-wives & mistresses!!
KEEF
©2011 K. Knight
Distributed by Universal Uclick for UFS
12/21

I'm in the red, so I'm going green this holiday season!!
"e-gifts" for everyone!! Cat videos!! Wardrobe malfunctions!! Dirty jokes!!
I think people want less stuff under their tree this year!!
I'd prefer less stuff in my in-box!!
KEEF
©2011 K. Knight
Distributed by Universal Uclick for UFS
12/22

CHRISTMAS IS A SHAM!! DON'T "BUY" INTO IT!!
CRASS COMMERCIALISM HAS RUINED THE TRUE MEANING OF THE HOLIDAY!!
YOU CAN READ IT ALL IN MY NEW BOOK!! MAKES A GREAT STOCKING STUFFER!!
SHAM
KEEF
12/23
©2011 K. Knight
Distributed by Universal Uclick for UFS

I was thinking about buying you a day at a local spa!!
Then I thought you might like a membership to the modern art museum!!
Then I was thinking: it's the thought that counts!! And that thought counted three dollars in my bank account!!
My thoughts exactly!!
KEEF
12/24
©2011 K. Knight
Distributed by Universal Uclick for UFS

COUPONS YOU CAN USE
COUPON
"MEAL EXCHANGE"
CUT HERE
✩ ENTITLES BEARER RIGHT TO SWITCH MEALS WITH OTHER MEMBER OF DINING PARTY
✱ APPLIES TO SALADS, APPETIZERS, ENTREES DESSERTS & FOOFIE TROPICAL DRINKS
CUT HERE
Value = priceless
KEEF
12/26
©2011 K. Knight
Distributed by Universal Uclick for UFS

Coupons You Can Use

"Do Unto Others.."
*Entitles bearer unsatisfied with service to **exact revenge**

"Gimme those scissors!!"

*Valid at barber shops, salons, make-up counters & plastic surgery clinics.

value = priceless

"Smoothie Run-Off"
*Entitles bearer to extra bit o' smoothie leftover in blender after filling glasses

← THIS STUFF

*...also applies to french fries at the bottom of the bag.

value = priceless

"Instant Lesson"
*Entitles bearer to one (1) instant lesson right then & there

"Show me how you made that remoulade!!"

*Valid with chefs, magicians, break-dancers, contortionists, musicians, surgeons, athletes & seamstresses.

value = priceless

"SINGLE FREE ITEM"

Coupons You Can Use

COUPON — cut here

* ENTITLES BEARER TO ONE (1) FREE ITEM FROM ANY YARD/SIDEWALK/GARAGE SALE

cut here — 12/30

"Thanks!!" "?"

* C'MON.. AREN'T THEY JUST GLAD TO FINALLY GET RID OF IT?

value = priceless

—KEEF

"FOOT RUB"

Coupons You Can Use

COUPON — cut here

* ENTITLES BEARER TO ONE (1) FREE FOOT RUB* LASTING **AT LEAST** TWENTY (20) MINUTES

cut here — 12/31

Grind Grind ♪

* APPLIES TO **BOTH** FEET (GRATUITY NOT INCLUDED ☺)

value = priceless

—KEEF

Every January 1st, I write the new year out 100,000 times, so I don't screw it up over the next week!!
Distributed by Universal Uclick for UFS
GIANT ROBOT
1-1
©2012 K. Knight
KEEF
Are you SURE you're writing 2012?!!
Or is it.. 1220?
ARRGH!!

COPS VS. FIREMEN!!
Are you pole dancers ready to forfeit tonight's charity hockey match?
Are you kidding?
Last year you ticketed the Zamboni driver & pepper-sprayed a referee!! I can't wait to see what you do this year!!
HA HA HA
HA HA
You better hope it doesn't come down to a shootout!!
KEEF
©2012 K. Knight
Distributed by Universal Uclick for UFS
1/2

COPS VS. FIREMEN!!
Why'd you bring me to a hockey game?
It's a fundraiser & an inexpensive way to introduce you to the sport!!
Hockey isn't just fighting!!
It's a perfect combination of balance, skill, power & finesse!!
So which team is which?
The cops are the ones in riot gear!!
KEEF
©2012 K. Knight
Distributed by Universal Uclick for UFS
1/3

COPS VS. FIREMEN!!
I think the firemen have a ringer playing goalie!!
Who?
Duane "Wall Street" Reade!!
Why do they call him "Wall Street"?
Cuz he's too big to fail!!
KEEF
©2012 K. Knight
Distributed by Universal Uclick for UFS
1/4

COPS VS. FIREMEN
FWEET
Tripping!!
©2012 K. Knight
1/5
5 minutes in THE penalty box!!
You can'T jail me!! I'm a cop!!
Distributed by Universal Uclick for UFS
So what am I supposed To do?
PuT me on administrative leave!!
KEEF

COPS VS. FIREMEN!!
Wanna go?
YeaH!!
©2012 K. Knight
A peace officer & a fireman going at it during a charity game?!! WHY?!!
Revenge for a cHeap sHOT.. Protecting THE goalie.. Sending a message.. Could be anyTHing!!
1/6
Distributed by Universal Uclick for UFS
I wanna drive THE Zamboni!!
No!! I wanna drive it!!
KEEF

COPS VS. FIREMEN!!
Dude!! THis is THe Scariest Sporting event ever!!
Don'T worry!! The ref is cracking down on players in THE second period!!
Distributed by Universal Uclick for UFS
©2012 K. Knight
Isn'T THis profiling?
9 of your Team's first Ten SHOTs in THe first period came from a .45 caliber weapon!!
KEEF
1/7

BLFFFTT
BLEAH THIS SWILL IS DISGUSTING!!
I USETA DRINK THIS STUFF CUZ IT WAS "IRONIC" & FASHIONABLE!!
KEEF
©2012 K. Knight
Now I drink it cuz I'm flat broke!!
Distributed by Universal Uclick for UFS
Poverty was way more fun when it was a lifestyle choice!!
KEEF
1-8

Distributed by Universal Uclick for UFS
You know where I'll be.. Feel free to contact me if problems arise!!
You be good while I'm gone, little man!! Don't hassle Daddy too much!!
©2012 K. Knight
1/9
I'm gonna miss you guys so much!!
Seriously? You're just taking a bath!!
KEEF

I read somewhere that putting epsom salt in the bath is good for you!!
1/10
©2012 K. Knight
It also said to put cucumbers slices over your eyes!!
And it noted that the Egyptians used milk in their baths for smooth skin!!
Distributed by Universal Uclick for UFS
ARE YOU SURE THAT ARTICLE WASN'T ABOUT CANNIBALISM?!!
KEEF

POP
Distributed by Universal Uclick for UFS
SUCK SUCK
1/11
©2012 K. Knight
Mama's having a bath right now.. You can have mi-mi when she gets out!!
Right now it's all about me-me!!
KEEF

Know what would be perfect right now?
knock
Glass of wine & an US Weekly?
A spouse with mental telepathy!!
KEEF
©2012 K. Knight
Distributed by Universal Uclick for UFS
1/12

I screwed up dinner again!!
No worries!! Steam some pears for the little one & heat up the leftover lentils with sausage!!
Earth's problems would be solved if it were run by 3 women in a bathtub!!
KEEF
©2012 K. Knight
Distributed by Universal Uclick for UFS
1/13

CRASH
BANG
FOOM
DRILL DRILL DRILL
BOUNCE BOUNCE
CRASH
SCRAPE SCRAPE SCRAPE
Okay--Now I'm worried!!
KEEF
©2012 K. Knight
Distributed by Universal Uclick for UFS
1/14

Life's Little Victories
New Parent Stylie!!
©2012 K. Knight
#1209: YER BABY TAKES A TUMBLE...
YIPE!!
CLUNK
WHEW
..AND HE DOESN'T CRY!!
YES!!
1/15
#1210: PUTTING SOMETHING HEALTHY IN FRONT OF YER KID'S FACE...
STEAMED BROCCOLI
YES!!
AND HE LOVES IT!
KEEF
#1211: SMELLING SOMETHING FOUL!!
UH OH!!
Distributed by Universal Uclick for UFS
.. BUT IT'S JUST A FALSE ALARM!!
HA!! YES!!
#1212: FOUR WORDS- SLEEPS THROUGH THE NIGHT!!
Z
YES!!
#1213:
WaaaaH!
YES!!
WAAAA
YER KID IS THE SECOND LOUDEST BABY ON THE AIRPLANE!! YES!!

My mouth hurts!!
When was the last time you went to the dentist?
1/16
Distributed by Universal Uclick for UFS
©2012 K. Knight
Uh oH.
KEEF

This toothache is unbearable!!
Sit in the chair so I can take a look at it!!
©2012 K. Knight
1/17
Ooh yeah... It's pretty bad in there!!
How can you tell?
Distributed by Universal Uclick for UFS
There are tombstones where your teeth used to be!!
R.I.P.
KEEF

Jiminy Crickets!! Your teeth are a MESS!!
Distributed by Universal Uclick for UFS
Do you realize that poor oral hygiene can actually kill you?
You've got to brush & floss twice a day!!
1/18
©2012 K. Knight
I do brusth twyth a day!!
With TOOTHPASTE, not BBQ sauce!!
KEEF

THE DENTIST!!
Next!!
That would be me!!
©2012 K. Knight
1/19
My chart sez there are two of you!!
My Dad is out in the car!
Distributed by Universal Uclick for UFS
Is he coming in?
He was hoping you had a drive-thru!!
KEEF

STOP!! POLICE!!
©2012 K. Knight
1/20
Why did you take off like that?
God told me to run!!
Distributed by Universal Uclick for UFS
I can't wait for the Republican debates to be over!!
KEEF

You sell diseased lollipops over the internet?!!
In a variety of flavors: "Cooties" "Heebie-jeebies" & "Mad Zombie"!!
©2012 K. Knight
1/21
Isn't that illegal? Who would buy such a thing?
You'd be surprised!! Sales have jumped 400% since October!!
Distributed by Universal Uclick for UFS
Wow.. There's a sucker born every minute!!
You mean there's a sucker SOLD every minute!!
KEEF

©2012 K. Knight
COOTCHIE COOTCHIE COO!!
STOP BABYING THAT BABY!!
Who are you?
I AM TIGER MOM!!
TIGER MOM REJECTS YOUR WIMPY WESTERN STYLE OF PARENTING!!
KEEF
1/22
Through endless badgering, pressure & THREATS, Tiger Mom had her kids SHOPPING for THemselves at your age!!
By THE TIME THEY were four, Tiger Mom had her kids ready to leave THE den!!
!!!
Wow!! Where are they now?
CHILD protective services!!
Distributed by Universal Uclick for UFS

A bird went to the bathroom on my head!!
That means it's your lucky day!!
©2012 K. Knight
PLUNK
Distributed by Universal Uclick for UFS
I didn't said it was **good** luck!!
1/23
KEEF

Whoa!! You never told me you had the Star Wars Blu-Ray collection!! How is it?
The films are great!! The extras, not so much!!
STAR WARS
Distributed by Universal Uclick for UFS
1/24
The extras are **bloated** with over **six hours** of useless, hard-to-watch blooper footage!!
©2012 K. Knight
Still in denial about the prequels, I see.
What prequels?
KEEF

KNOCK KNOCK
Coming!!
Distributed by Universal Uclick for UFS
©2012 K. Knight
Hi Keith!!
Hey!! It's my cell phone!!
Yup!! You keep on losing me.. but I keep on finding my way back!!
YAY!!
1/25
You are **SOOO** smart!!
THE REALITY
BEEP
KEEF